"You know, that might be the answer – to act boastfully about something we ought to be ashamed of. That's a trick that never seems to fail."

- Joseph Heller

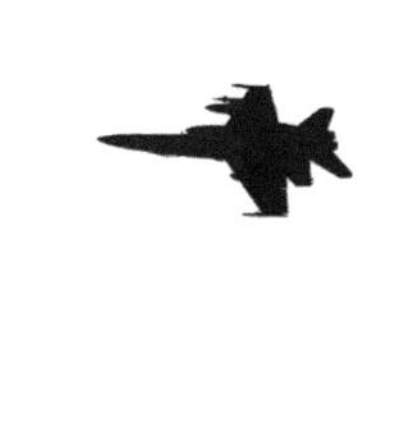

These poems explore memories from one military enlistment in the U.S. Navy.

agape.guru is an anti-brand. This space, this period of time, this collaborative collection of matter seeks creative ways to connect people in need with places that grow seed. Rebuild the House of Wisdom.
"It starts within."

pseudonanamous poems
written during Warrior Writers
workshops, with a gang of clowns

ISBN: 978-1-7348401-7-9

Ghost Post Press

ISSN: 2770-0518
Boston, Massachusetts, USA

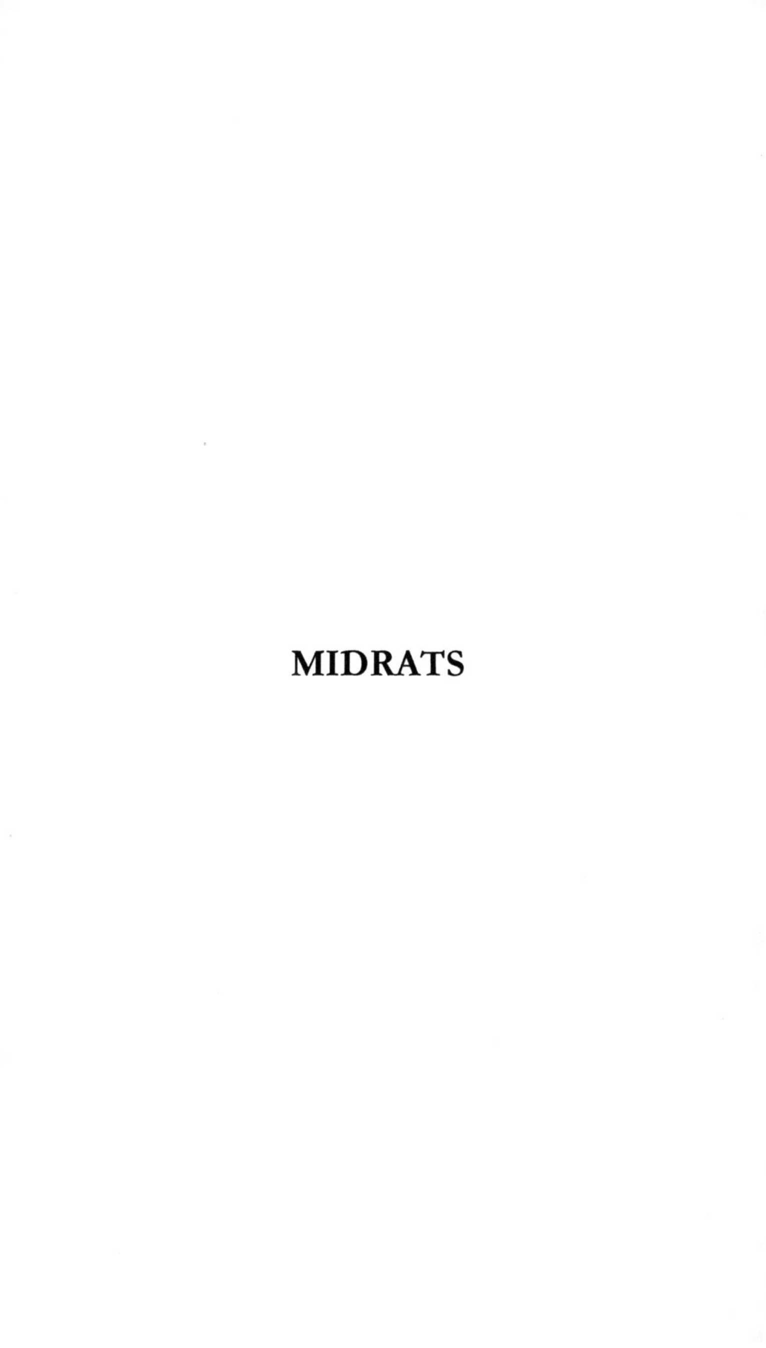

MIDRATS

Catch 22

When I said I was going to join the army,
forget journalism, I'd become a helicopter pilot
she stepped on my toe and said, "If you die,
if you get killed, I will hate you forever."

So I went to a madhouse, and examined why
I might want to die. Why do I want to kill
somebody? While I was there, I met this
addict, this fiend, my desirous deviance.

When I returned from the asylum, her mom
warned, "Don't throw stones in a glass house"
and we broke up. She called it temporary,
but she plants grudges like flowers in a cemetery.

Rats Also Ate Joe Brainard's Book

I remember rats scampering behind the line at dusk, between the dumpsters, under the smoke pit, stuck, screaming on glue traps, drowning in toilets, in barrels of Turco, doused in JP-5 with a flash point too high to light with cigarettes or matches, harassing us airmen for bits of our boxed lunches while we detached for another week of target practice.

I remember nights on watch when the coffee maker bubbled while the sun stained the sky in regal gold and pink and red and purple, dropping behind the runway, as beautiful as infinity, falling into another desert night under constellations and constant cold dry longing.

I remember the petite pilot in the bar with short brown hair and bright eyes, who grabbed my arm and said she remembered my face but forgot my name. I remember that being the first and last time I saw her.

I remember emphatic rebukes, drunk wrestling and boxing matches. I remember a friend suggested I write something happy. I remember random uniform inspections to fill time and shame out shitbags, to check our attention to detail. I remember burning off IPs in the smoke pit.

I remember my fuck buddy calling from the beach to break up, and I remember caring about that.

I remember feeling sorry for the dead-eyed people, especially for the timid boy shopping with his mom's oxygen tank, and his mom yelling toward him every time he dropped his hand from her cart.

I remember breakfast at the casino, eggs served by strippers, rides to the NEX.

I remember watching Nicholas Cage ride a motorcycle and brandish a whip. I remember a lot of sucky movies.

I remember flatness and deadness.

I remember the artist tattooing a phoenix on my chest for seven hours. I remember he said he had a light hand. I remember the jaw numbing silence between his monologues about how girls blow him for free tattoos and the ethics of fucking sheep.

I remember he said that sheep vaginas feel like human vaginas. I remember smoking a cigarette every 30 minutes, and how afterwards I shook like a rattlesnake slithering out of a cold cave to bake on a desert rock.

I remember walking along barbed wire fencing, kicking tumbleweeds, sucking on a lolly pop and feeling its sugar coursing in my blood. I remember thinking how so many of those trailers looked abandoned, and how much work must be done to fix this place. I remember a lot of busiwork and so many jobs not getting done. I remember loving the dry heat.

I remember standing in line outside the liquor store waiting for a truck to unload fresh beer.

I remember hungry fiends surviving in the allies, looking wasted and old, and the rats lurking under cardboard box flaps, redeyed. I remember not knowing this place, and judging it harshly.

I remember barbecues at 3am, after flight ops. I remember that one girl on base who didn't belong to a squadron, who worked at the NEX or something. I remember punching through a screen to bust my friend's lip.

I remember my friend who said he fucked the girl from our sister squadron who I'd hollered at on the Line. He said he felt like he was raped at a barracks party because he caught feelings, but the girl was just using him for fresh dick. I remember thinking he was bullshit.

I remember to not tell stories that are not mine.

I remember oily curls bouncing on the crown of the SEAL who sprang upon us like Dionysus with his three friends circling in like jackals from the darkness, drunk and scrappy, celebrating some intense training, showing off a tribal salamander tattoo, calling himself a loaded weapon, making me want to fight. I remember how a girl from my shop saved me from humiliation by inviting him into the room to play games.

I remember towing jets from the line to the hangar and back. I remember there are five pitot static moisture traps to drain with a flat head from door three. I remember checking the oil. I remember how sweet hydraulic fluid tasted when it filled the belly of my jet and slid around my eyeball like lubricant. I don't remember how many times I got the shits.

I remember chains and tie downs.

I remember driving tractors down deserted runways, doing doughnuts full throttle at midnight, kicking up dust. I remember breaking things and fixing them or not. I remember being moody.

I remember how the lights on our jets appeared like gods from the stars, blinking red and green and growing apart. I remember the strobes flashing, and the bounce, and the lift, and bashing on the tarmac, those hot and smokey hydraulic hops, whenever the birds landed.

I remember heat in my earmuffs and goggles, dry eyes blinking, ears leaking wax. I remember the pop of the sweat when it poured from my noggin, walking through the warm exhaust, and the coolness of the air when I took off my crainial.

I remember exploring empty aircraft control towers.

I remember nights on watch when the lights blinked.

I remember the gruff voice from the black receiver, cold to my ear at two in the morning, "Don't tell anyone, not even the Rover. Log this."

I remember the Rover popping his head into the ready room every half hour after to say, "ALL SECURE." I remember logging each entry in our green "RECORD" book.

I remember the white plaster walls in the Ready Room. I remember the steel desks with formica tops. I remember the white linoleum and grey carpets. I remember the pictures of the CIC, CO, CMC and so forth. I remember manilla folders piled on the desks. I remember the dry erase boards, and the dicks people drew on them. I remember the excitement rolling in my gut for hours when I kept the news fresh and silent all morning.

I remember that phone call that dictated a log entry, now buried in that decade old book that also says "All Secure" every half hour marked compulsively every two lines without incident. I remember a helicopter crashed into electrical wires, incinerated during a training mission. I remember they were enroute to Texas where some of their families waited. I remember "five aircrew dead."

I forgot their names until now, since I looked them up. I remember the officer on duty spelled them out slow: "Commander Shehan, S-H-E-H-A-N, Lieutenant Anderson, A-N-D-E-R-S-O-N, AW1 Weatherford, W-E-A-T-H-E-R-F-O-R-D, AW2 Rosetto, R-O-S-E-T-T-O, and AW2 Bibbo, B-I-B-B-O."

My journal entry from that night says the pilots trickled into the ready room about an hour later, and one asked me (oddly), "Are you ok?" I remember saying something stupid like, "Yes, sir. Are you?" or "Yes. Bad news, sir." And he said something like, "I don't understand why he was flying so low at night." I remember someone said he was always a crazy fucker. I remember thinking I got a scoop.

I remember, we could not get rid of those rats. They followed us even months later, skittering up the moorings to meet and mate with Greek rats and Arab rats. Some rats even ate my clothing. When I got off the boat after cruise, I remember throwing my books in a dumpster on the pier, with my greasy flight deck jerseys, thinking the rats could also eat these.

Shipping Out

Pleasantly hungover, methodically clicking
on my signal, peeling the lid off a last pint
of vodka, glancing in the rear view, avoiding
the attention of the MAs, sipping, turning
in the lot, thinking what I forgot. I need to buy
new shower shoes, an hour until muster,
pulling up, parking, battery sparking as
I unhook the cable, slam the hood, strap
on my sea bag, lock the door, look back
briefly, scanning my park job, how my car
would sit for seven or so months, turning,
tramping down the lot, waving at shipmates
pausing to adjust my shoulders, falling in
and out of lock step, all of us swarming
toward the ship, families saying bye on
the sidewalks, at the geedunk while I avoid
long conversations, rush by, bye, decide
to stop one last time to buy a hamberger,

some last shore food instead of shower
shoes. If they're sold out in the ship's store
my next poem will be "Athlete's Foot."
Meandering from one line toward another
along concrete barriers as the headlights
of traffic leaving Norfolk flick on,
I watch the last pink and green sunset
fade behind the rows of destroyers,
walking up the pier toward the line, up
the gangplank, into CVN 75. 15 minutes
till muster, already ready for my rack,
queasy 'cause tomorrow we pull out.

Waiting in the Catwalk for Recovery

The ocean rolls eternally
or might as well. What I see
is several billion light years
of blackness beyond the beam
of my industrial flashlight, up
past a seabird flapping, past
a cloud puff, probably past
some satellite my light
particles pass in waves still,
maybe toward a distant planet,
diminishing at the inverse
square of this time and intensity,
photons dissipating, so dim an alien
peering up from the deck of another
nuclear vessel so powerful
it destroyed its own planet
and now floats clear
of the fallout, on another desolate
gulf between great masses
of stone and grit, this
survivor looking up whose eyes,
maybe a million lifetimes more fit
to transit this universe,
still won't observe me

wiggling this odd, irrelevant
signal of meaningless motion
a wave so profoundly
speedy, flying faster
than anyone ever
on and on and on.
The horizon is a haze
where the stars start
like static, like a steamy
snow globe, like so many
pixels sliding so slowly up
from the ocean, like so
many sparks trailing
in the atmosphere behind
Prometheus bringing fire
down from Olympus, trailing
sparks in such slow
motion I can't comprehend
the vastness of time
and out of the stars
a trident of lights glides
growing in intensity
red white and green
spreading, pylons empty
and the oxygen combines hot
in molecules clapping
to crescendo in my cranial
in the sweat in my headset
shaking my ear fibers as our jet
formation flies by.

Jocko Willink's Rules for Success (as a wave poem)

When things go bad, good things come.
Got beat? Good. You learned. If you're still
breathing, well then hell. Get up. Re-
load. Re-calibrate. Attack.

Discipline is the root
of freedom, of flexibility, of intelligence.
Discipline your ego so you make good decisions.
Face your fears. Control your desires. Discipline
calls for strength, and fortitude, and will. It won't
accept weakness. It won't tolerate another
break down. Discipline means taking
the uphill road, doing what helps
you and your team.

You want to improve? You want
to write a book, to make an app, to sing, to be a SEAL?
You want to get better? Where do you start?
Start here. When do you start? Start now. Initiate
the action aggressively. You go. The idea
isn't executing itself You have to do
it now, so get after it here. Stop
debating and just do it. Take
that step.

Strength is weakness.
So, me? I am weak. But I don't accept it.
I don't accept that I am what I am and that
that is what I'm doomed to be. No. I'm fighting.
I'm struggling. I'm scrapping, and I'm kicking
and I'm clawing at those weaknesses to change
Them. Sometimes I win. Sometimes I don't,
but each day I get up with my fist clenched
toward the battle, as I struggle
to be better today.

In college I read
every book assigned. I sat down and forced
myself to read every single page of every single
thing. It's almost stupid. It's almost a waste
of time. Lock that brain down and get it
done. Boom. Laser focus.
Report. Done.

One instinct to look out
For, this lier, this saboteur, this backbiter,
like the devil, a shapeshifter, disguised as your best
interest, this instinct says you've done enough, you can
stand down, you can take a knee. Do not listen. It wants
a place of sympathy, a place where all of these failures
can gather in comfort and drown their sorrows in lies
and deception. They tell you it's ok to settle.
You need to smash those
into the ground.
Fight on.

Millions of warriors have faced evil
and faced death much worse in other times
and places, in much worse situations, Gettysburg,
or Vicksburg or the Battle of the Bulge, and all
of those horrible situations, they prove
that you can withstand unimaginable
stress. You've got to detach.
If you can't control
something, embrace
what you can control.
Stop worrying about
what you can't control.
Don't fight the stress, turn
it on itself, use it to make
yourself sharper
more alert.

Do it
when you don't want to. When you say
I can push it off a little bit, Jody
wouldn't accept that answer.
Don't self talk. Don't say
I'm going to do this
or I'm going to do
that. just do it.

How do you step
into bravery? Step. Step. Take
the step. Step aggressively toward
your fear, and that step toward what
you don't know, that simple action,
that simple attitude, answers with
bravery. Mitigate the risk,
and ease into it, you will
overcome your fear.
But take that first
step to inoculate
yourself against
the fear in your mind.

When you practice
any skill set, when you train,
you get it. It's something anybody
can get. Practice
every day
for that decisive
victory.

Terror Is

Terror is the young Hydra your neighbor keeps feeding
Terror is the rabid bat in your bedroom.
Terror is the needle in your daughter's night stand.
Terror is the tumor metastasized, a social worker planning
your funeral.
Terror is the chambered bullet.
Terror is the eyes of a fiend in the darkness.
Terror is the hungry pit bull on the corner.
Terror is broken glass under foot, your baby sobbing.
Terror is your baby taken.
Terror is your uncle's car exploding.
Terror is bombs blowing up around you.
Terror is teenagers with machine guns.
Terror is famine.
Terror is plague.
Terror is daddy drinking with his Glock on the dresser.
Terror is the theistic monomaniac, the suicidal slayer who
wants his spirit to live on.
Terror is the byword of the kamikaze, and let's not forget
that a suicide bombing is still a suicide.

Ship, Shipmate, Self

I hear terrorists took pot-
shots at our passing battle
group, but nobody saw them.
We laughed at the dents
patched up after hailstorms
and the wind traveled as well
particles of gas colliding, at odds
knocking each other. Air itself sounds
like far off fighting, and the mechanics
making it move under the helicopter
overhead that shits oil with such
torque. And our boat 'staches
full of grease and oil, caught
the fish-sick smells
of the Suez mixed
with nicotine
and chunks
of non-skid.

Watch that Egyptian
officer in the dune
buggy riding parallel
escorting our ship. Here,
take my binoculars. Look
at at him pick his nose, peer
at his sandy mucus as he flicks
it out the window as his dune
buggy bounces. Does this not
feel like a movie? See each
of the four flags flapping from all
four corners of the transport that follows
him. Stare at the way those two men you can
see sitting on the sideboard hunch over their
weapons, and note the relative thicknesses
of their moustaches in the shadow of that
arched canvas. In one second those six
or whatever warriors could be
nothing but flesh and shrapnel.
As they rush along, sending up a trail
of dust, the driver's sunglasses gleam
as he looks toward us, one hand
on the wheel, hair flowing to a peak
like it's full of gel. Gold bars
on his shoulder glint in the sun,
and the antennas on the hummers
ahead of him jostle wildly.

Focus on the rigging, and those
vehicles blur into the dunes while silver
lights refract sunlight in kaleidoscope
patterns across the deck, where
the white sand whisps
up sometimes like ghosts.
Bone dry sand smells
like a playground, and down
on earth here the manure smells
sour. Eyes closed here, now, the softer
effect of the news copter rotates through
a blanket of leaves rubbing and rustling
together, green like the limes
in the lemonade
on this picnic table.
Listen to the cars pass on the street
at the bottom of the hill, from The Dojo.
The sound of traffic and the clickety train
the far off rumble dissolves under the sounds of birds.
What does each sound mean? So much chatter.
Who feeds the twittering sparrows,
who flock across the garden? They rise
like curtains in the wind, and flow: "This way,
this way, they sway." The sound of all the people
around me writing makes my mind talk meanly.
We're drunks. We're cowards. We're apes mapping
out brief and inane trials on paper. I record
my sniffles, my breathing, my heartbeat.

Dear La David Johnson

The Army says you ran fast
for cover, that you were known
for popping wheelies, that you fought
to your death alone under a thorn tree.
I imagine you died standing.
You look so young
in those videos the Army
made. Always skeptical
of news, of official narratives, of the truth
viewed through a mirror, darkly, I know
human foibles can be beyond belief.
I remember how segregated
the galley would get, and a lot
of casual racism on cruise.
I imagine, not a green beret,
maybe you were an "other" too.

I believe you existed, even
though all I've seen online
is your image, like the opposite
of a mugshot. Your real experience
is as blank as the space between
your eyes under that maroon
baret. I imagine how the line
formed for photos, after drills,
to be remembered for this brief
political moment. In the hierarchy
of deeds, yours remain unknown,
and you will also be forgotten
next week in another blizzard
of doubt and discontent. Meanwhile
your wife will be home, baking cookies
for visitors, taking calls.

Violating The Red Zone

The call crackles forth, "Slingers up,"
for an FCC to Cat three, Starboard. Off
the rubber static guard, out on the Port side.
Catapult one scrapes back, so they're launching,
no crossing the flight deck now. Steel digging,
knuckles chafing, grey box swinging first
through the passage, propelling me past
the library: secured for ordinance in the El. Back
aft, past ready rooms, to a Boatswain who blocks
the way, wet deck, wash job, waves
me off. Down another passage, down
three flights, through the hanger bay, past the wet
paint watch, up three decks, past the gym, out
on the Starboard catwalk. Saline wind tickles
my cheeks after the hatch sucks air around me
and I step out into pure darkness, smell the Grapes,
slide over a fuel slick, feel the ladder rung through
my boot, press the FCC finally up to the non-skid.
Blood flows back through my fingers. Fuck. The Red
Zone takes shape to arm the bombers. Down,
from below the darkness smells like rotten
socks rise from distant foaming wave breaks.

The invisible Gulf, full of dead TVs and broken
binders stares blankly back at me. On the ladder,
Flight Control Computer digging through my thigh,
waiting for the opening, looking up at Virgo flying
high over the Hydra. Connect the dots. On deck
Red lights flash. Fuck the AOs ritualistic
bullshit. The pins aren't even pulled,
and our pilot is about to miss this launch
over a short. Hop on deck. Lope toward
the waving red bulbs, feel the rush
through my teeth as a loaded
fighter turns in for service, lights up
my eyes, and I race like a fiend
on acid, violate the line. Chief grabs
my float coat collar, smacks back
my cranial, "Dumb ass." I leap toward
Cat three, head first into the abstract.

Orange

Sunsets fool with waves in the Gulf.
Dark in divots, cresting orange,
like aluminum foil wrinkling,
reflecting a broiling sunset,
under smoke and clouds glowing bright
with oil stains, ripples the water.

Colorful flashes of water
light a straight path across the Gulf
from this carrier to the bright
horizon, splitting an orange
porthole, or another reset
button, its bottom half wrinkling

into a trail westward, wrinkling
in time, a battle line in water
for the fly in from the left. Set
a course up wind across the Gulf
as they approach in the orange,
just back from bombing Iraq. Bright

night lit deck, I climb up bright
faced, glancing beneath me. Wrinkling
in waves of brown and dim orange
under the catwalk that water
churns and froths at the hull. The Gulf
disappears after the sunset.

Donning crainial and headset
as flight schedule begins in bright
flashes and sparks I cross a gulf
now dark, running with chains wrinkling
on my Camelback, guzzling water,
wet eyes, ducking under orange

orbs, avoid exhuast. Orange
beams bathe the deck, a smile set
around my teeth, with salt water
saliva dry in my cheeks. Bright
flashlights find tie downs. Hook wrinkling
chains up to the jet, in the gulf

of a wheel well, and set bright
orange safety pins, an inkling
the pilot wants water in the Gulf.

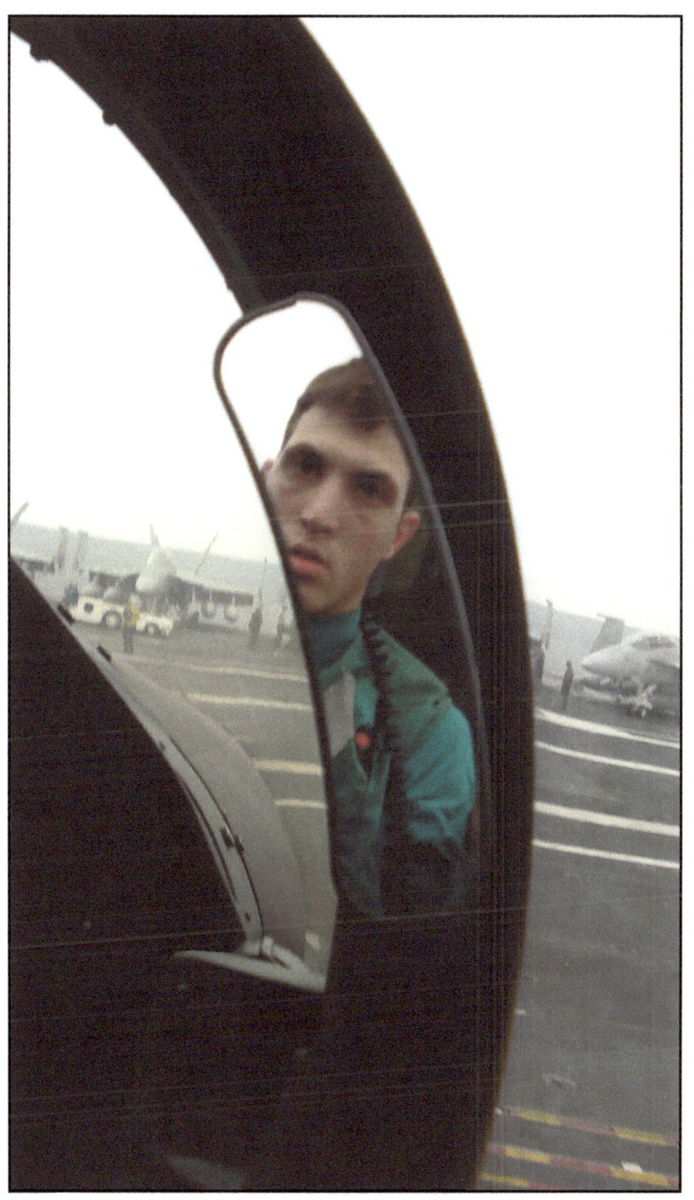

March 28

Pastoral Bound in Steel

Tramping up the ladder I knocked my knee
It broke where a scab had barely formed
Blood coated my pants, gushing free
I kept walking ignoring the gray throbbing
To miss the pipes my skull was bobbing
I found myself in a head

The toilet paper in the stalls was gone
So I pressed my sticky pants to my knee
The leaking stopped, it didn't take long
I peeled my cammies away from the wound
I pulled my pantleg up its knee ruined
Bloodclots make fabric hard

I waddle in puddles and dropped on a c[illegible]
The steel stall around me fogged in places
Someone had carved a cock
All over the words Fuck the Navy slowing its lo[illegible]
The contradictions hung heavy
And a pipe dripped on me

I don't think I quite understand a pastoral. It is meant to show beauty and gayity. I can't even parody it well.

USS PASTORAL

Spangles wave on Brave bombs under blasphemous jets While the sun also sets

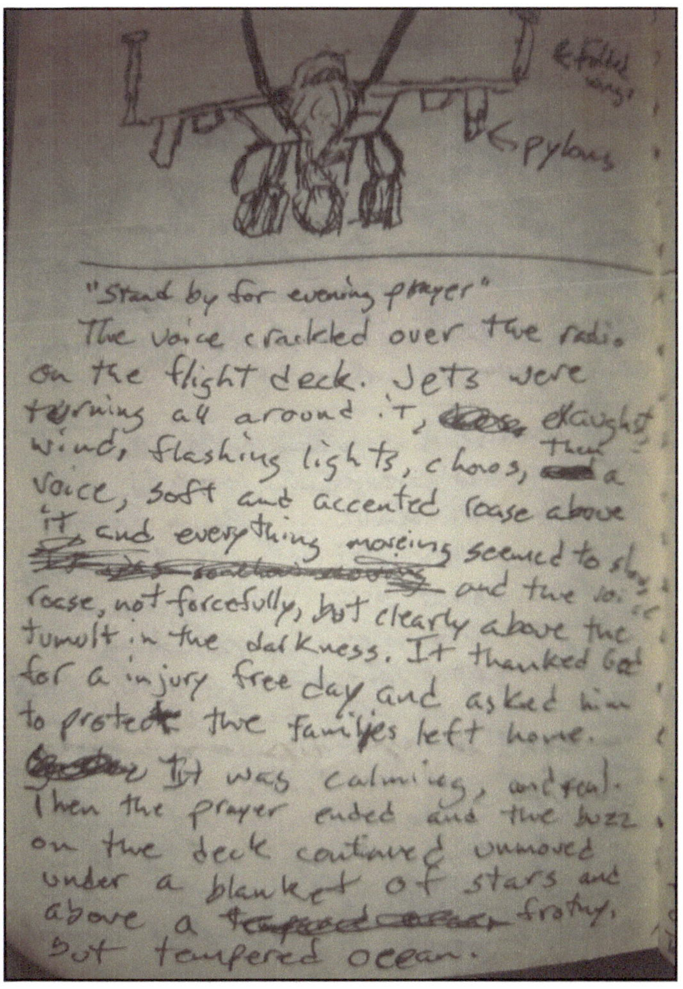

"Stand by for evening prayer"

The voice crackled over the radio on the flight deck. Jets were turning all around it, draught wind, flashing lights, chaos, Then a voice, soft and accented rose above it, and everything seemed to sl and the voi rose, not forcefully, but clearly above the tumult in the darkness. It thanked God for a injury free day and asked him to protect the families left home. It was calming, and real. Then the prayer ended and the buzz on the deck continued unmoved under a blanket of stars and above a frothy, but tempered ocean.

1.

"Write a letter to an enemy," Brian Turner said at the Old Oak Dojo.

Leaves whispered violent nothings over a cohort of Warrior Writers gathered around picnic tables in Boston. Notebook paper flapped against a pen scratching out first thoughts to Tarek Mehanna.

Now serving 17.5 years in prison for Material Aid to Terrorism, Mehanna translated troubling documents that "Promised [certain holy rolling gangsters] firm establishment on Earth and dominance over the people of disbelief."

Combining language from the Dojo with stuff from journals kept in the Navy by a young Aviation Electrician's Mate striking up a conversation with Mehanna through the mail, this concrete poem is set in transit between the Mediterranean Sea and the Persian Gulf. In form the poem honors nostalgia and naval expeditions, contrasts the aesthetics of nationalism against nature, and salutes those working to rebuild The House of Wisdom.

Spangles wave on

Spangles wave on includes lines by (1) Faleeha Hassan, (2) June Beer, and (3) Vo Que and explores nationalism and the mighty emotions involved in a sea passage.

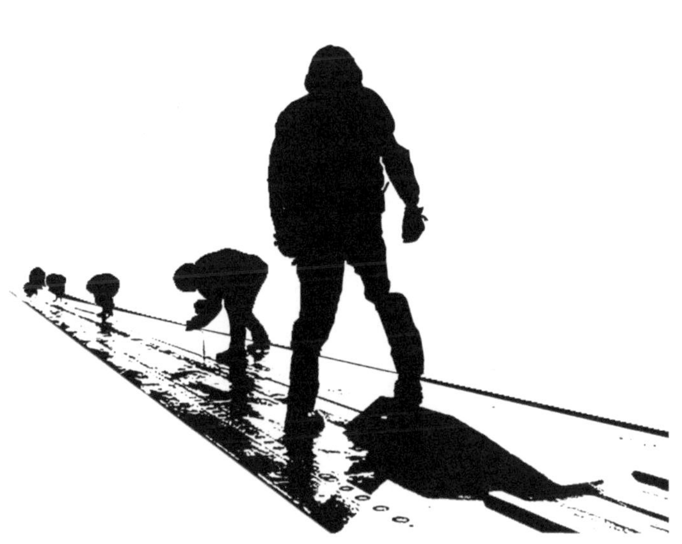

practice my loneliness[1] half the peach[3]
un poema de amor[2] O B E A U T I F U L
as the steel shivers glowing in waves A M E R I C A F L Y
wrinkled redness
colors shift while fish schools fly U P O N H O T A I R
bathes the hecktic
D A R E D E V I L S
they repair to airborn aliens
swells, wine lit waves S C R E A M P A S T
the gunwale thin as eye floaters
glimmering over ghosts see seabirds dive & cloud,
underway algae glows pestilent-pixies
granite-faced braves peck at fish-nets, fight
bright and shifty
with sharks below watch as Mars appears in flight, tear guts apart

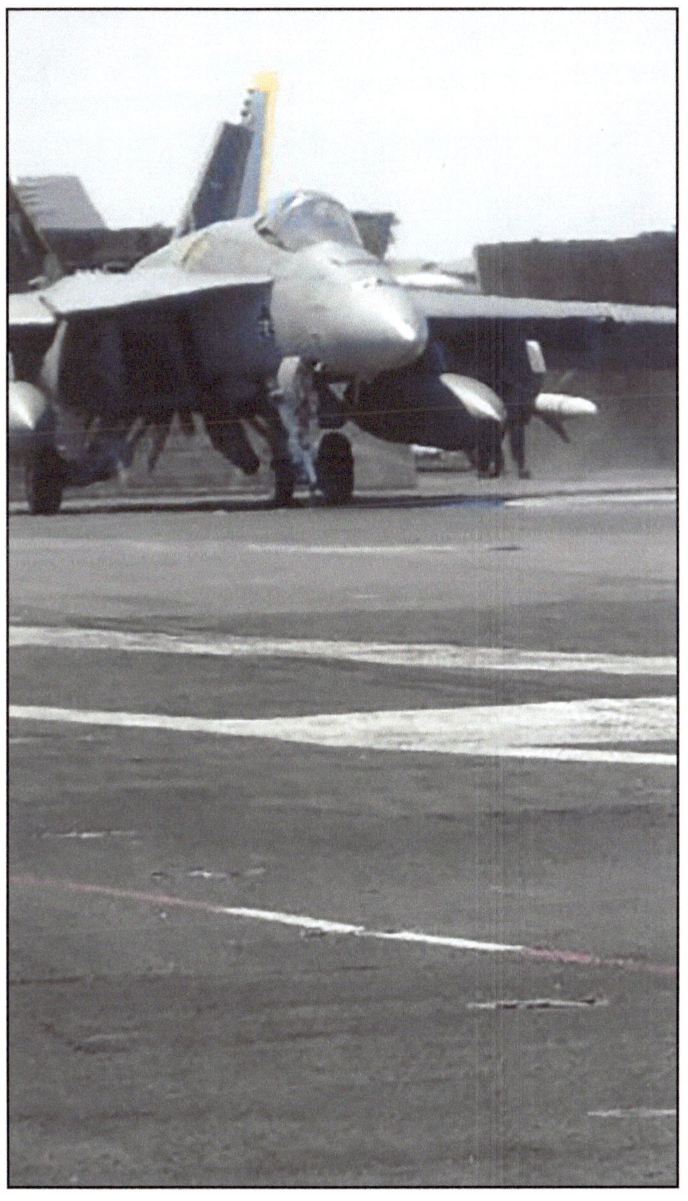

March 24

Severed Cock

All I've thought of today are cocksuckers
Cocks for everyone's mouth
Balls dangling on chins
My Boss
With a long veiny member limp between his teeth
Just a bunch of severed cocks
Dangling out of foamy mouths
Nawed on
Because people love being noticed.

I want to sleep forever

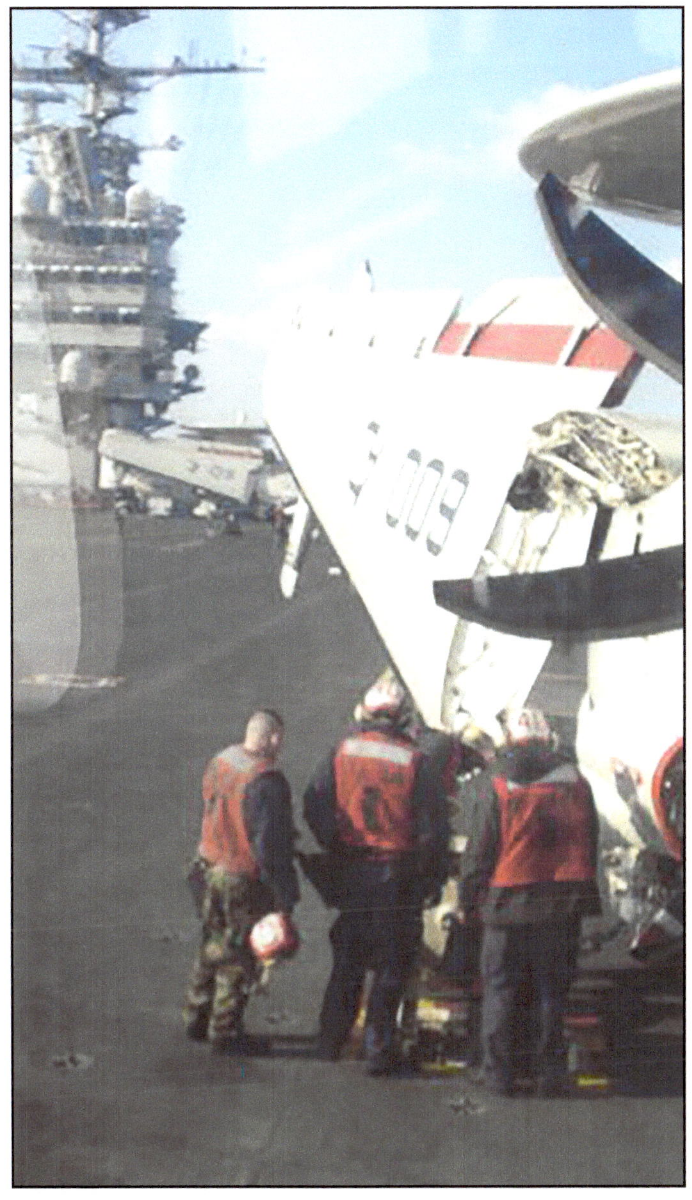
009

2.

“Rebuild the House of Wisdom” is an esoteric call to action, recalling the translation efforts of the golden age of Islam, before the Huns sacked Baghdad. Referencing wars past and present, this card aims to connect people across time and space and to inspire constructive conversations between enemies.

Frontline Arts imprinted the USS PASTORAL poem in three parts on Combat Paper, made from old military uniforms. Emphasizing image over substance, the concrete form follows Gregory Corso’s poem “BOMB” and reacts to the view of a famous journalist who observed, we are “guided by the beauty of our weapons.”

Images of ordnance overshadow the narrative of “one war everywhere” motivating theistic monomaniacs into suicidal conflict. We seek agenticity amid chaos. We tell stories to create a sense of cause and effect that sometimes seems traceable, logical, understandable. But often the truth has plot holes.

Brave bombs under blasphemous jets

Brave bombs under blasphemous jets assumes the form of an F/A-18 fighter jet to contrast ancient stories of war and adventure with our modern conflicts.

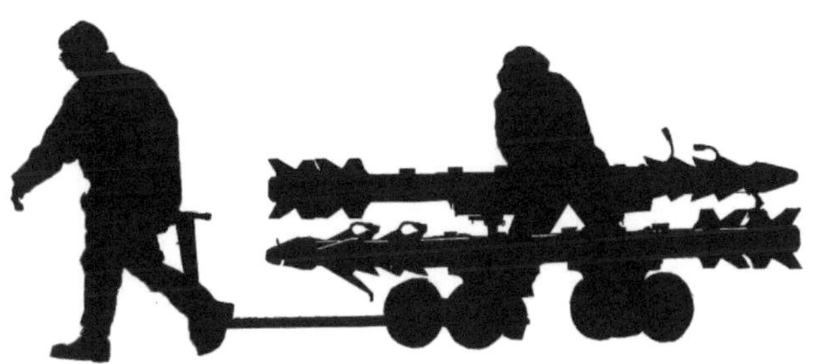

IT'S A BIRD
IT'S A PLANE
A FLIP BIRD

God, gold in the gloaming
blends with
blue to misty
bourbon foam.
Walloping waves
peak and pocket:
black, bright, below the birds
floating in airflows up high, up
against Ra, orb of war, slipping low so slowly
aft. As we turn, pacing in The Gulf, circling, awaiting
orders to bomb a desert depot, or secure some patch of sky, as far
away as Afghanistan. We can refuel midair, circumnavigate the globe, so good luck
escaping our fury. Our battle group could obliterate civilized society, the fallout would be
spectacular. Glass breaks under boots in Babylon, where Daniel woke with lions. Meanwhile, at scrub-x
we clean the tracks after our jets subjugate, slaughter, steal away in a silky sunset, spining up orange circles,
leaving tangles of dust rising at the earlier end of night-ops. Waves bash without rhythm.
Oil fires dance like brass-spangled skirts around Al Basrah. Chains
jangle, grease glittering, wet deck night lit. Shadows dangle
Bathsheba's veil over the genealogy
to Sindbad's treasure. The prophet
left a vote: Bakr or Ali? Do we fight or seek
diplomacy? The Jihad (since the walls of Jerusalem fell)
defines invaders. Against airflows
the fighters shriek.
A short wire
chafes as
cannon strafes.

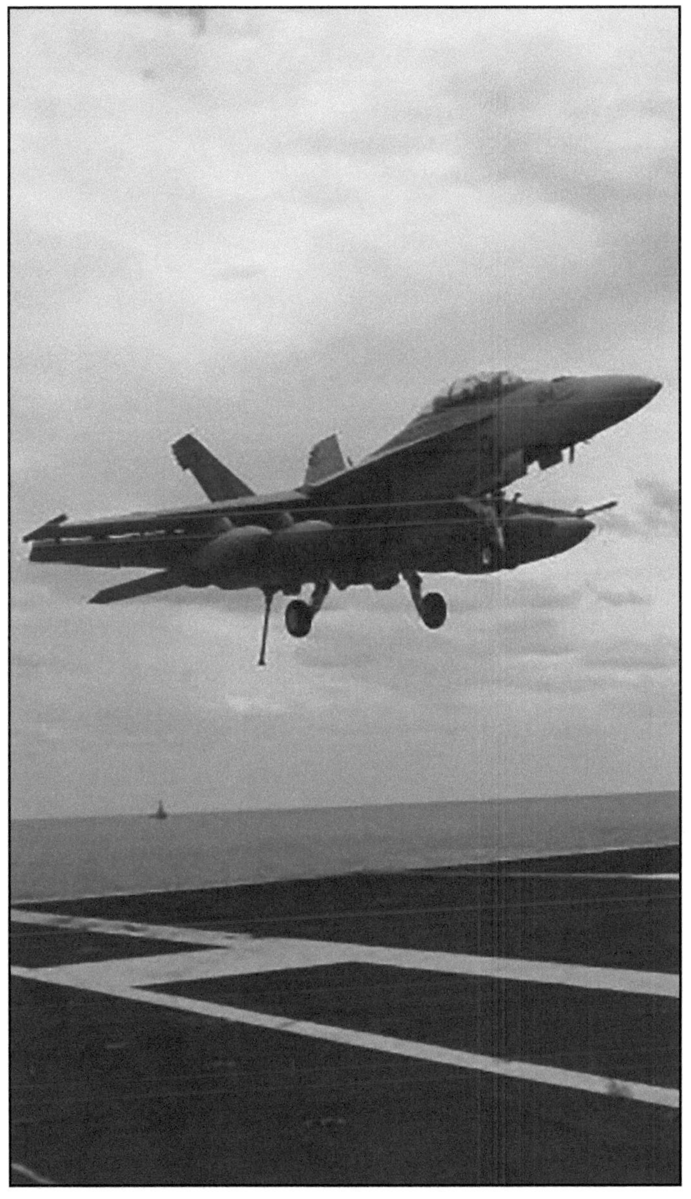

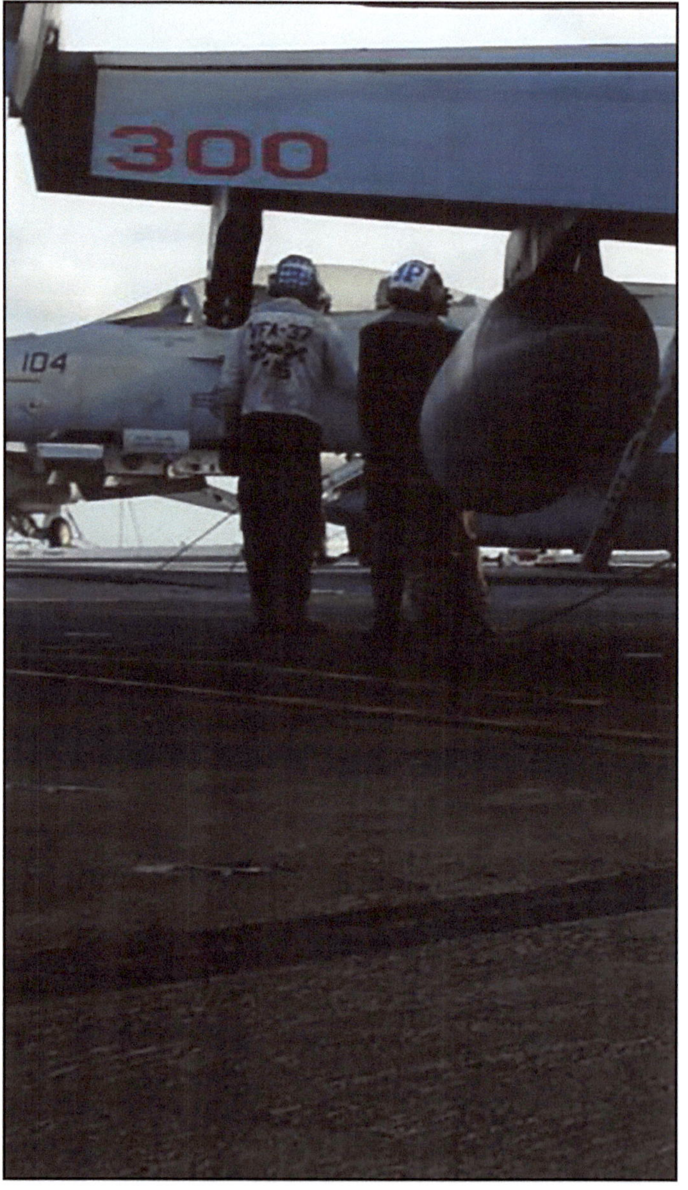
300
104
VFA-37

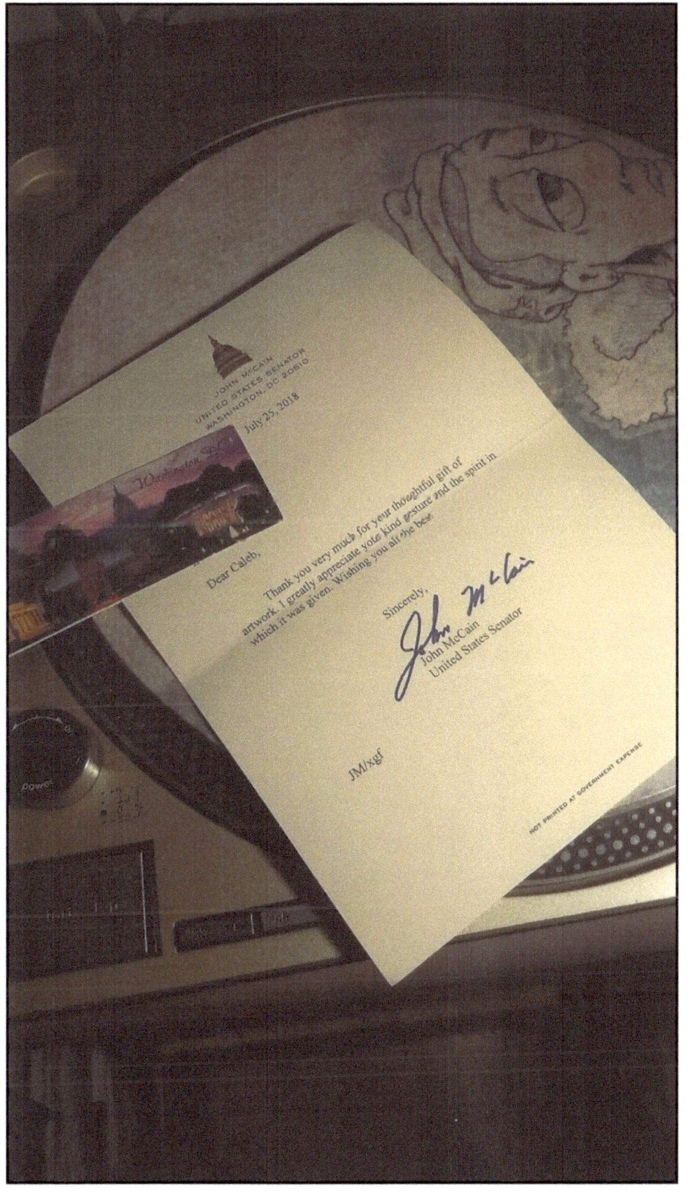

JOHN McCAIN
UNITED STATES SENATOR
WASHINGTON, DC 20510

July 25, 2018

Dear Caleb,

Thank you very much for your thoughtful gift of artwork. I greatly appreciate your kind gesture and the spirit in which it was given. Wishing you all the best.

Sincerely,

John McCain
United States Senator

JM/xgf

NOT PRINTED AT GOVERNMENT EXPENSE

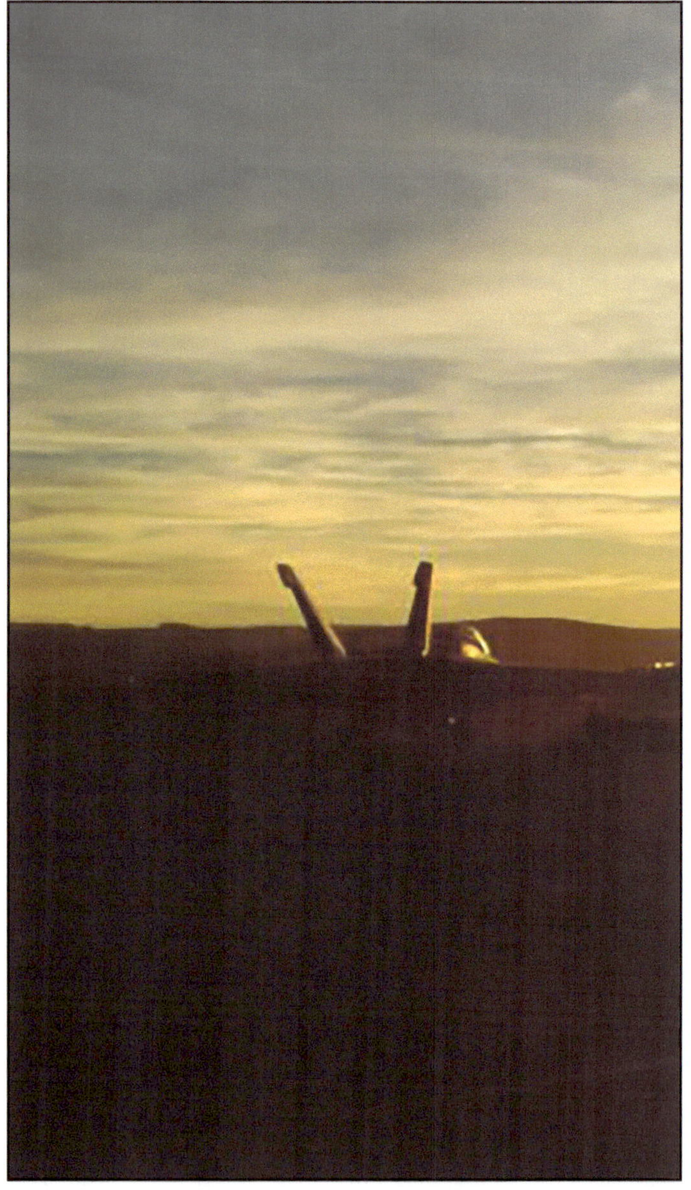

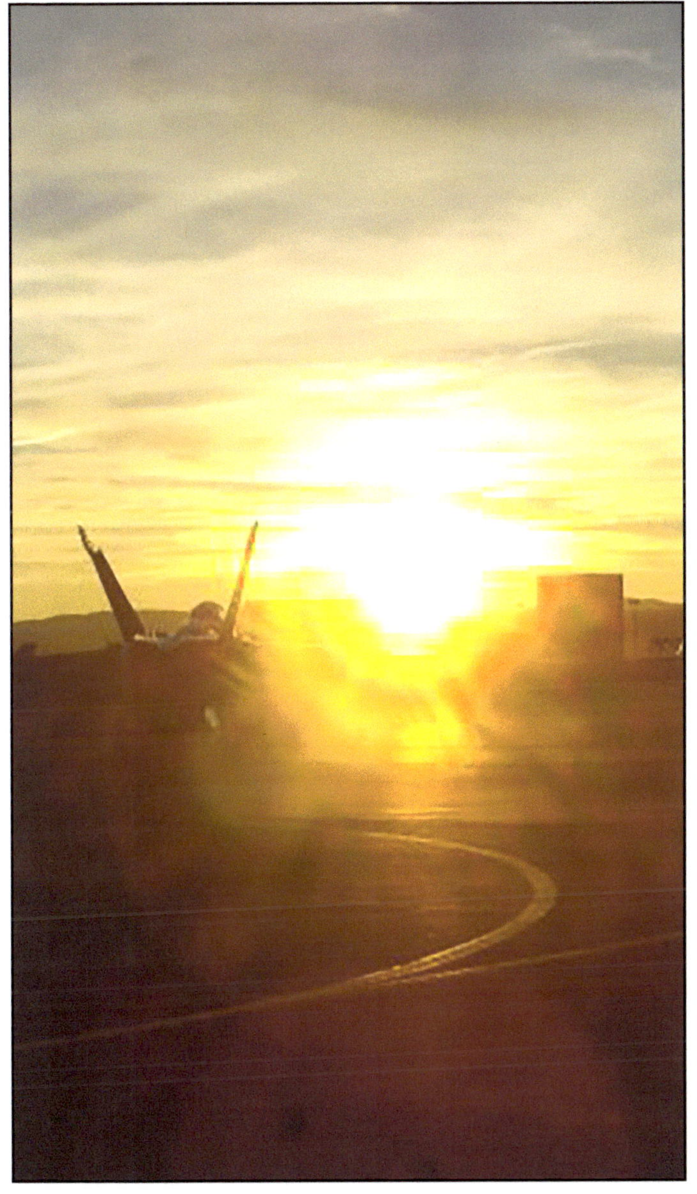

3.

Propaganda, Edward Bernays' famous tract says, "Universal literacy was supposed to educate the common man to control his environment. Once he could read and write he would have a mind fit to rule. So ran the democratic doctrine."

Designed with Bernays' ideas about "social machinery" in mind, this concrete poem uses apophenia and pareidolia (our tendency to see patterns in unrelated things) as a form. Our actions, choices, more than words what we do, how we use our time defines our values.

Former Navy pilot, John McCain wrote in his Letter To The United States, his final formal words, "We are citizens of the world's greatest republic, a nation of ideals, not blood and soil. . . . We weaken our greatness when we confuse our patriotism with tribal rivalries that have sown resentment and hatred and violence in all corners of the globe."

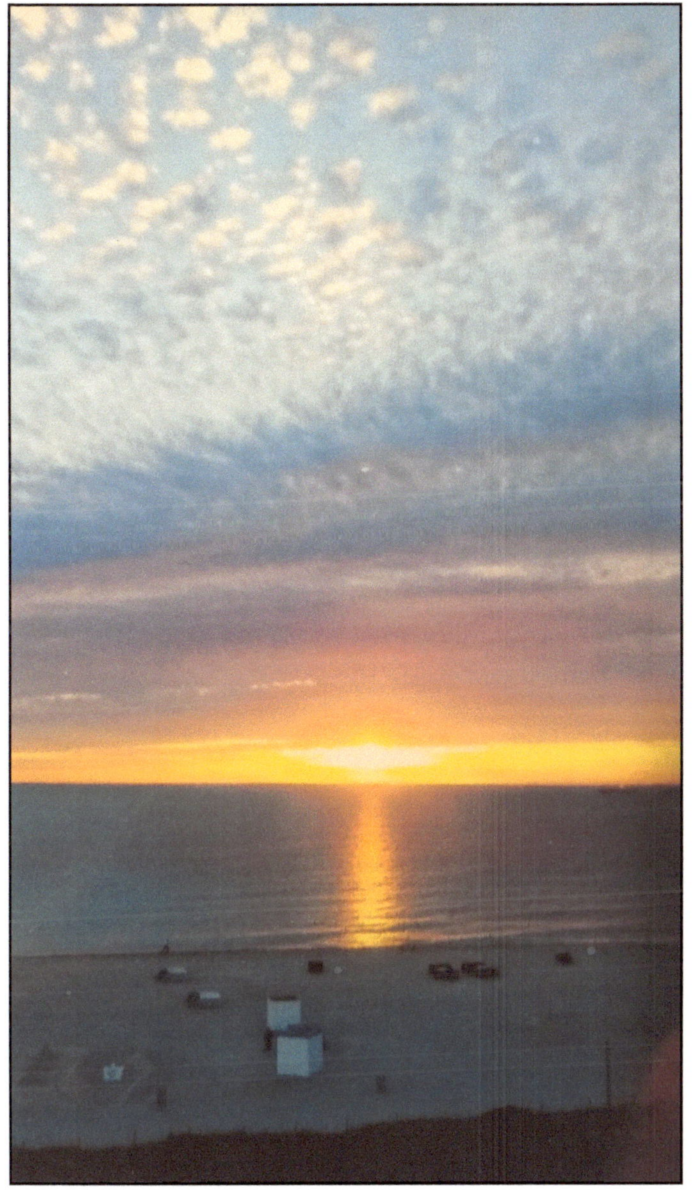

I hope you've been well.

It's been interesting reading of your experiences in the Navy, so thanks for the letters you've been sending.

As for me, I'm doing well. To answer your question: no, there is no window in my cell.

To answer the question you've been repeatedly asking implicitly: yes, there is meaning & purpose to life. Don't lose hope.

Let me know when this reaches you.

Take care,

[signature]

While the sun also sets

While the sun also sets inspired in part by (4) Derek Mahon, adds some discordant textures to the sights, the sounds, the smells of cruising on an aircraft carrier in the Persian Gulf.

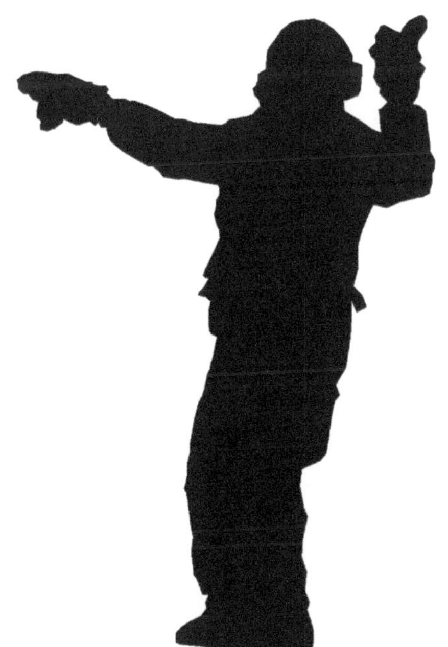

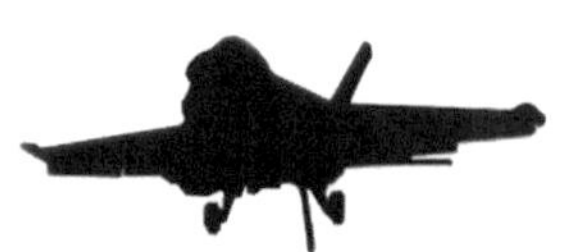

Sun
setting or rising
on the horizon, trailing
light West or East, grasping
net below deck in the smoke
pit I see the porthole to hell.
Knocking on steel, the exit latch grinds. I feel its echo reverberate through my subconscious.
The door behind creaks,
thuds again, cycling smokers. The engine rumbles
through my feet, hatch moans
amongst orange sparks streaking.
Ponderous waves grow and go
rippling with spurts of gold, below the noisy sky.
I watch the shadow of the boat sharpen
or dull, dissipating into night or dark in feverish light.
In the shadow, wind-whipped neck itching,
jersey billowing
out, I blow smoke
over the snot- yellowing waves.
Formless clouds
upward haze, not stormy, not even a suggestion of rain,
just defuse water, a Gaussian blur.
Purple and pink shades of
pastel colors run across the sky.
The sun's direction realized,
rising white or setting out of bloody
sight, everything morphing bright
or black, night-lit ochre,
ghostly, jets scraping the deck.
The ocean rolls out and oil rigs blaze,
flick, flit, dance about all day,
all night, over cylindrical pipes
spouting red from the water, flaming
like apostates in ancient cities.[4] Life lurks
near luminous plasma, sole fused by gravity,
always exploding. The sun also sets on depravity.

www.ingramcontent.com/pod-product-compliance
Lightning Source LLC
LaVergne TN
LVHW052309100826
845147LV00006B/717

* 9 7 8 1 7 3 4 8 4 0 1 7 9 *